CITIES OF MATHEMATICS AND DESIRE

AND OTHER POEMS
1988–2004

CITIES OF MATHEMATICS AND DESIRE

AND OTHER POEMS
1988–2004

Judith Emlyn Johnson

THE SHEEP MEADOW PRESS
RIVERDALE-ON-HUDSON, NEW YORK

All inquiries and permission requests should be addressed to:
>   The Sheep Meadow Press
>   P. O. Box 1345
>   Riverdale-on-Hudson, NY 10471

Designed and typeset by The Sheep Meadow Press.
Distributed by The University Press of New England.

Printed on acid-free paper in the United States. This book meets the guide-
lines for permanence and durability of the Committee on Production
Guidelines for Book Longevity of the Council on Library Resources.

Library of Congress Catalog-in-Publication Data

Johnson, Judith Emlyn.
    Cities of mathematics and desire, and other poems, 1988-2004 / Judith
Emlyn Johnson
        p. cm.
    Includes bibliographical references.
    ISBN 1-931357-97-8 (acid-free paper)
    I. Title.

PS3569.H44C58 2005
811'.54--dc22

2005001296

Books after 1985 (published under the name Judith Emlyn Johnson):

THE ICE LIZARD / poems 1977–88: Sheep Meadow Press, 1992

HUNGRY FOR LIGHT: The Journal of Ethel Schwabacher (co-edited with Brenda S. Webster) Indiana University Press, 1992

Books 1968–1979 (published under the name Judith Johnson Sherwin):

Poetry:
URANIUM POEMS (Yale Series of Younger Poets Prize 1968)
IMPOSSIBLE BUILDINGS (Doubleday 1973)
THE WASTE TRILOGY (Countryman Press 1977–79):
    THE TOWN SCOLD (1977)
    TRANSPARENCIES (1978)
    DEAD'S GOOD COMPANY (1979)
HOW THE DEAD COUNT (Norton 1978)

Fiction:
THE LIFE OF RIOT (Atheneum 1970)

Non-fiction:
LITERARY AGENTS: A COMPLETE GUIDE (Poets & Writers 1978)

Audio:
THE TOWN SCOLD (Watershed Tapes 1977)

ACKNOWLEDGMENTS

I am grateful to the editors of the following periodicals and anthologies, who accepted for publication the following poems, some of them in different forms and with different titles:

The Other Side, "In the Opening Night Sky"; *Exile,* "Cities of Mathematics and Desire"; *Southern Lights,* "The Lava Tree"; *Chelsea,* "For Margaret, Grieving"; *St. Andrew's Review,* "For James, in Time"; *Frontiers,* "Quiet Life"; *The Paris Review,* "Magna Mater"; *Poetry Society of America Newsletter,* "The Logic of Teacups"; *The Massachusetts Review,* "Press Conference"; *American Poetry Review,* "Moonscape"; *For David Ignatow: An Anthology,* "The Invasion of Lark Street, Albany, After the First Bush Inauguration"; *Legacies,* "Stone Olives"; *Virginia Quarterly Review,* "As if I Watched Late Last Night with Baudelaire"

I am also grateful to the Poetry Society of America, and to Robert Creeley, for giving an early version of this manuscript the Alice Faye Di Castagnola Prize.

for my daughters
Miranda, Alison, and Galen

TABLE OF CONTENTS

Coda:

Notes on Typography:

This volume uses the symbol | before a line run-over to indicate that the line is part of the preceding line rather than a new line indented.

The symbol / is drawn from the scoring practice of Charles Olson. Like the caesura used by Gerard Manley Hopkins (which is not among symbols on the ordinary computer keyboard), it indicates a non-syntactical or musical pause whose length varies according to the amount of blank space surrounding it.

IN THE OPENING NIGHT SKY

love, we are all born out of this holding darkness
into our lives
                    down a bloody current,
and against our wills we rejoice in the light, we are grateful to breathe;
the air fills our lungs, the light fills our eyes,
the tenderness of the earth fills our skins
                              the gladness
                              of touch,
and we swell with it, we give birth to ourselves through the world of sense.

full of ourselves, we never see that what we hold inside
is that darkness which nourished us before we knew our minds.
                    when we feel the rich undersea
                    cave awash with our salts
we grow afraid, we pull back, we hate entering again
          to find that life out of which
                    with such struggle
                    we broke;
and, although when the wave lifts us and slams us inward,
          we ride, jelly and weed inhabiting our pores
we dread good Mother Night who bore us and whom we bear.

ONE:
CITIES OF MATHEMATICS AND DESIRE

CITES OF MATHEMATICS AND DESIRE*

1. Wargames

One night last year worn out, half asleep
on the subway, back from Albany to visit New York
where once i lived, i caught from the corner of my eye
      a ragged, filthy street tough who stood with his back
        to me and leaned his fist on the map near the door,   5
           cursing a nearby sleeper.
          His black leather jacket,
  which, because his loud voice drew me, i turned to see
  straight on   /   was slashed through in four deep stripes
    right shoulder to left hipbone. He opened his hand   10
    and pressed his palm to the map / the nails black, untrimmed.
When he turned to shove the teenaged lovers at his back,
    who'd just gotten on, i saw,
full face now, the purple bruise over his eyebrow
    the narrowed eyes, the lips pulled back.   15
The few late night travelers rippled back from him as from a
                      |thrown rock.

Something in the way the light slanted past him
or on him, or his deliberate look, hands on hips now, elbows out,
as he cast his shadow over the scattering passengers,
like the shadow   /   of a two-bladed axe, reminded me   20
    of the one i had loved so much thirty years ago
  and spent twenty years losing, of the way he leaned
    forward, his distant frown like a surveillance
    satellite   /   hovering over the chessboard.
        He said that to win you had to hate everyone   25
            you played, and i, in his energy, heard,
            not   /   singularity, but fine excess.
        He spoke of the game's

---

* See note on typography on page ix.

beauty as a lover does, or a prophet,
as if a bishop move at the right time could open 30
jammed subway doors, a queened pawn could lift stuck
| elevators,
and a sacrifice in the tunnels under Times Square
could make an oasis bloom there, could make the Neva rise
to whisk you away from a death-trip street-gang, could call out all
the loaves from Park Avenue to Hell's Kitchen, and hecatombs 35
of fishes up from Galilee to feed the starved.

2. Of the Power of Chess to Feed the Starved

If straight lines from need to done, if playing by rule
move grain from Iowa to Biafra, if pure science chart
trajectories from want to fill or pure
art rename the world to its will 40
these Long Island bluefish that scatter in random flight,
should, at my call, leap to shed their chemical residues
in a clean fire, sequin Brazilian shantytowns
and rebuild lost Aztec cities in the South Bronx.
With the glitter of broken glass and prisms, of rainbows 45
making a jeweled court robe of their fins, their scales,
they pour up out of that generous water
whose surface also, rippled by the desert wind,
weaves a glitter of half moon arcs and laughter
interlocking, repeating each other to the circling shore, 50
a diadem so far away that we'd lost all sight of it.
When we cast our nets   /   not needed, because the fish are ours
and leap to us as if drawn by magnets,
the small water-beads
coating the half-moon meshes echo aloud, 55
laughing, shouting curses underground.
The rippling scales,
and the cirrus clouds spread, dimpled on the blue sea above us,
take up that laughter, throw it back in our faces.

5

[Dialog of the Cirrus Clouds and the Bluefish]

Like answers like, their laughter says,   60
      (these clouds that will be shredded to rain
      before i lie down again in a lover's arms).
      Because the sky is a net, and the dimpled water
      a net, you are caught and can't escape.

                  But the bluefish   65
      all buck and flurry   /   pulled by that current
        whose laughter is a curse   /   fling back at them:
like answers like, yes. *Because we are caught*
and will be stripped by the flat of a knife
our half-moon scales popped up in waves   70
the sails of our fins stripped from us, our needle
spines lifted from the flesh they owned,
                (though that flesh
                keep still printed deep
                the ripple of our bones   75
                as we pass
                through the world's huge mouth,)
you are caught in that self net. The steel
crest that draws its line between flesh and bone
will cleave you like a propeller's blade, leave   80
a wake deep enough / and so / wide
galaxies pass through. Though we don't swim
the Neva here, and the lost don't come
like Akhmatova's, at your summons, when the drops close
behind you their deep ravines will still cleave   85
in every molecule's code the maps of being.

3. Of the Power of Maps to Predict Milk

i thought then of love's power, i who have known
    what it is to lie all night in bed with a carnival

phantom, a masked bandit,
to kiss lips that melt at my touch   90
from flesh to the cold glass / of a picture, a mirror,
to open myself   /   like a wave, a two-bladed axe,
and be entered and filled /   by a jet of air, a lie
that our longing shaped / not by a passion;

i who have known too in a different city   95
how nerve can be strung to nerve so strongly
steel cables are less, and an ocean between not break them,
how bodies once bound, and minds and wills once bound,
if they hold, when they part can bend all space
paper-flat, compact all heat to their single measure.   100

You, networks of subways / who tie the far
reach of Queens to the Lower East Side;
you, hidden, dangerous silks, who bring my daughters home late
nights from dull, dead-end jobs to world's-end dreams;
you, webs, hammocks   /   who cradle the hungry   105
child and its worn out mother, back from the clinic,
equally in your rocking, even while you ferry
the smalltime hood from his room to the street where he'll make
his kill; you, maps of my city's fury
and hunger; you, underground, be my synapses, my maelstrom.   110
Carry the farthest galaxies close where we can touch them;
link the pawn to the box it lies down in so the cost becomes
                                                         | clear;
tie the sacrificed queen to the hand that plays her out
for a cause not hers; the Neva's swirling smoke
to the Gulag's masque of forced confessions; the coiled   115
computer-tape paper profits to the missed
payments and foreclosed mortgage; the industrial grade
diamonds to the blazing tire necklaces and the slave towns
in plundered South Africa; the abandoned cesium
in the obsolete x-ray machine to the man and the woman   120

7

in the dusty village, hungry for a moment that shines
like an Andean god, and their dust radiant forever.

Knot cause to effect so that those equations burn
the gap in our minds, as an infant's distant cry
still pulls me from sleep and makes my breasts ache   125
with remembered milk as if to my daughters' night howling,
even now they're grown women, as my loins crest
in an empty bed remembered heat and milk.

City of lust and city of mathematics
the four diagonal slashes on the roughneck's black leather   130
sliced through to grip his back with black-rimmed nails,
death's strong hand clenched in a lover's flurry.
    Late West Side streets whose moonlit walks
uncoiled thirty years ago: how many lovers'
heels they've tasted since and still not full?   135

[Song of the Times Square Graces]

Generous under the young moon
let's tide together. As Boulder Dam
leans to the Colorado's torrents;
as downstream generators hum
to plunging falls that make them burn;   140
as bulb drinks current; as Broadway drinks glitter;
my breast drinks power under your palm.

As hotel lobby, cruised for pickings
near dingy station, soaks up numbers touts;
as jammed elevator soaks up all patience;   145
as grease-stained walls soak up boy and girl
who hurry and greedy and heedless flurry
glued close, slide hand up under blouse;
as grifters love any free show;

my belly rows, weed and sway, to your thighs.   150

We that have lava to keep us blazing
can spare an atom of love's coin.
The river that pours its fury to dazzle
cities, won't spend half so freely as we.
When No-Holds-Barred *leaves* Love-Me-Tender,   155
the world will sell tickets to watch us die.

       ★   ★   ★

             Just so / at the fulcrum of our lives
we promised to live generously as the river/
            so / the elevator,
      that should have plummeted down at our call,   160
              remained stuck somewhere
        between the twelfth and the eleventh floors/
so / we climbed to our one-hour room /
            so / a jungle throbbing
            like a bluefish cathedral   165
            in some Aztec hollow,
               | galaxies north of Brazil
           felt the Arctic air pull, felt
the Monarchs tremble in the heart of their vast cloud.

4. The Flight of the Monarchs

Dappled under the shifting leaves
first one, then another, gilded flakes that sift   170
through steam layers, they stir their wings.
Like snow that filters down through the bare fingers
of oak and ash, they ripple up through
summer and rain, the tangle of vines,
wet, heavy air, green weave that would hold them fast   175
to familiar grounds. All color and darkness,

gold, black, they lift. Their waves leap, span
oceans, flow north to my lordly Hudson

                  and span it too.
Though they travel, not in one cloud   180

                but in small bursts,
                particles of mottled
                and jeweled light
                shot from the swirling steam
                as if from an accelerator,   185
          their passage is a wave.
Compress the space between, we'd see them soar up and outwards
across the Hudson like cables of the high bridge
whose silver strands reflect the river below.

[Dialog of the Monarch Butterflies and the George Washington Bridge]

Line, span and cable, their wings cry,   190
(those wings that stroke summer's air, but one day
under glass will spread open from bodies pinned down to felt
                          | matting),
   hold us together as you hold
your city and its opposite, don't let us splinter
or lose our single motive force   195
that has pulled us from so far away.
Though we've come to the Hudson, not the Neva or the Seine,
   though there are no heroes to lead or follow,
   though the wave of our flight be invisible fire,
     so scattered you make its curve guess, not graph,   200
that pulse is our life. Without it we melt
and become only a powder raining down
our gold from dead wings.

    But the span shoots back,

the line you fly, though at its crest
it is a rising, all one flow,
breaks at the height. The separate drops
fan out and are sprayed apart. I, gravity's whole,
free arc, see how you will be pulled
away and away in a widening curve   210
till the one of you does not know its other.
All connection will break. Not until
dead autumn wake and the leaves feather
their spirals for the long sifting down,
will one of you in the curling   215
shadows feel sister call to brother
and lift before the snowflakes gather.

5. The Scholars of Chaos

City of moves and city of mathematics,
under your streets equations plot and spell
intricate star-charts.   /   Exact ratio, they mirror   220
    my chess-player's passion: how queen and pawn, exuberant
                            | variation,
    to him might have been /   as numbers, shape and true
                            | measure,
          divine change, were
    to world-shifting Archimedes,
          dovetail, pattern,   225
          combination, not combat.

Though you haven't come to the Doges' Palace, nor even
the marshes west of despair, the Groote Markt in Brussels
          where once i thought i'd won love back,
    not to any fulcrum you need if you'd move the world,   230
    not to a dimension outside time and space
    where the polar star rains in radium crystals
    up from the tundra's snow, and the amber day

preserves forever its single ruby drop
in a petrified embrace; though this is not the Lethe 235
nor sand-grained Ilium
but my own city   /   where crumpled bag-ladies
sleep on gratings, where a wavering
translucence from the subways
warms those whose link 240
with reality has torn;
though this is not
infinity but the place of zero clearance---
you, number of the arc, interweave, ornament, spin,
you, to whose measure the heavens 245
ring music from dust of exploded
stars, pure science of names who as your syllables
call things they must be,
now tell me
what might you do with love's words 250
to rename this world?

Even such a universe of pure play, of glee
and baroque remaking i thought i'd found
and loved in him i lost. Though that universe lied,
and neither of us moved to the other's measure 255
if ever i found such focal light again,
wouldn't i spread its wings and nail it fast
to a black felt mat, encase it in six
thicknesses of diamond so hard and bright
not a drill of fire nor a whirlwind 260
driven by a maniac's hand wielding a nova
could pile-drive through,
to shiver that deep center?
Those chess-club nights written in invisible blood,
win and loss lay over each other, 265
coincided   /   as circles with the same diameter.
Checkmated king and sacrificed queen

                corresponded   /   as mirror to image, as self
                    to double, as nature to temple, as lover
                    to lover, not one less needed, both equal.   270
They balanced   /   the way dancers, one lifting,
                            holds the other in flight
                            at the moveless point
                            before the downswing takes them,
                    the way the great Russian poet and her son   275
                            in a station, he bound for prison
                            or slaughter, she left alone
                            with dread in a ghost house, spun
                                                        | free,
                    the way light-rays rung in a mirror,
                recoil   280
                        angle of incidence, angle of reflection,
                        each where its symmetry sends it.

That web, economics   /   aesthetic
                    of generosity, not tenet
                    of parsimony, a single gong rung / to one   285
                                            | hammer
i in my eighteen year old bones
thought i could keep one whole, clear tone forever.

Unmeasured, the shifting curve: how the storm-clouds fray up
in threads of water pulled out from misted roads,
how they hover a while and linger over the blacktop,   290
bodies, stirring gently in long, slow coils,
in washes, curtains with fronds, palm fitting itself
to breast, thigh sliding over belly and down over thigh,
and then up again, how they knit themselves together,
until the air changes, makes knots, tightens itself   295
around its invisible center. Fanned by invisible wings
the clench of water and air begins to turn around itself:
spiral of computer-tape uncoiling from the market floor.

It lifts, opens, widens, pulls more clouds in,
and more, takes flight, sucks in sand particles,   300
insects, leaves, newspapers, rattan, canvas lawn furniture, rocks, cars,
roofs, houses, yanks rivers up by their hair over levees,
drills corkscrew dust-serpents through,
torrents down, flattens cities.

[Dialog of the Tornado Drill and Chaos]

Down, cities of greed and meanness, the storm-drill drums   305
      (that fury which freely spends itself
      and winds down in careless entropy).
        Though your roads knit door to door,   / and bank
        to the starved for whom no door they'll ever own
        or dream their own will open,   310
   you have lost
      hold of the nets that tie you one to another.
   You are sucked up
      out of your lives, dust to a vacuum,
      fish to a cannery,   315
and do not feel each other die.
What will you say when the fury you have called from the core
of the living dust funnels down on you
and your selves are rushed up, pulverized, star from star?
How will the particles that lived know they are dead,   320
or the parts of the dead re/fuse themselves from chaos?

But chaos, answering that gambit, throws back:
   you, tornado, weigh no more than a pebble in my hand.
   The pulse that pulled your water-drops
   out of the sweating ground, that grooved   325
   ravines deep with your jackhammer rape,
   i fanned
      and drove with a single butterfly's wing
        That wing I touched

> was so far away
>> its flutter so minute,
> that only my frozen scholar,
>> studying strangeness, alone in a silent room
> can measure its spin that can't be seen, its charm
>> that won't stand still, can plot it
>>> not by itself
>> but by how when it stirs
> the air somewhere else / corrodes.

6. Sheba's Apron

City of lust, city of particles
whose speed and location burn equally beyond my graph,
what can we know of these small units,
measureless desire, / who should be held, each to each,
> but who race centrifugally away underground
these variations, furiously escaped from all others,
unaccountable perversity / vehement, random force?

Do we truly believe that they / mirror each other,
> that because i place one / here
> on my grid, its companion / severed
> in a nanosecond's slice, in a word's throw, by the erasure
> or the negative inversion / of the universal cohesion, split
by my thought, flood, ocean, tsunami, my holocaust,
my Nagasaki, my death-camp, drawn by the vacuum
out of the whirlwind
> / none the less
>> will copy
its every terrified quiver, pulse for pulse?

City of untrammeled will, not the Palace of Golden Bulls, not
| Knossos

330
335
340
345
350
355

of the tangled path, but my own home:
    it so happened, jerked by chaos
        or chess, we got off 360
        at the same stop, that El Greco
        Cucurucu Angel in black leather,
        and i, yanked in his footsteps,
        up from your tangled bowels like sour air.
  It happened by chess   /   Apollinaire in the London fog 365
        yoked his Czars and Zaporoguean Cossacks fast
        with metaphor's irrational force
        to the woman who refused him;
  by chess   /   the lament he forged helped shape this poem;
  by chess   /   LeRoy Breunig, scholar, thirty years ago 370
        taught me, his student, to map this music,
        so drew this line, from Apollinaire through me,
        to Akhmatova in her masqued rhetoric,
        those connections she wove of her own loneliness,
            a nation's torment, 375
      with the stanzas the censors cut, kept
          white space whose voids blaze invisible ink.

  Now gravity, the mute core
    that holds us, self to self, unclenched, breaks.
The street tough shot off one way, i another, 380
two particles with the same charge, recoiling,
and i thought of the chess-player i'd loved
and bore children to, our broken vows, our lost honor,
of how kindness in the end lay stretched so thin between us
    that it shredded, and love itself sat down at the board 385
    to play one dull waiting move after another
till we ground each other down.

[The Revolution Talks Back to Apollinaire and Akhmatova]

No, i am not Sheba's lethal apron

from whose strings Nerval hanged himself, not Fata Morgana,
false show of flame, not Vesuvia with her fiery farts,   390
not Hecate's bosom   (though i wear a brooch shaped
                              like a bat, an axe, a pinned butterfly)
                              not the Death Hag
                              in your mirror, the other
                              to your death wish,   395
 nor Gloriana's false teeth and hair
nor the white rice powder that covered her pox
when she knit her nation to a strong chain
while the Great Armada scattered
                              like a cloud   400
                              of Monarchs at an axe-breath
                              of exuberant air.
Nor can i, a fog jacket worn by a hoodlum
       stagger out of a tavern, drunk,
       grab Apollinaire by the shoulder, belch: 405
                     i'm the one you followed for so long.
                     All that time i was the one you waited for
                     to return, to fling my arm intimately
                     around your neck, breathe into your mouth
                     before you could pull back in disgust   410
                     while i tell you what lies in store;

No, nor can i, a mask and a stone glove, hiding
the rebound from the future / weave woozily back with the other
                                                        | ghosts
      to pound on the past's door /   where Akhmatova, grieving
                                                   | conçierge, waits,
       as i shout at her: *change it, change it /*   415
                          this is the Revolution speaking;
                          if we leave it as it was, we'll all
                          rain down in dust.

Though i've not knocked, and they're dead,

theirs was a different future. It wore   420
a different revolution in a different
house on a different street. I'm not the one
pounding at their door. Instead
that stone guest knocks still, mine to answer. Such as i am,
i'm here, in my house, the voice of my time and place.   425

7. In the Palais-Royal with Gerard de Nerval and Others

If ever i forget what love was like
let my feet turn heavy, malignant rock,
    my mouth be fused obsidian.
If i regret spent years, lies and grief,
let Times Square's tunnels rise,   430
    knot themselves around my throat,
let the winch that turns round the polar star
ravel me vein from vein and squeeze the threads
    through a needle's eye in the Milky Way.

We, less wise than a madman's play, did not   435
keep on walking love's clockless West Side streets
together, hands joined, as in the Palais-Royal, that clear-tongued
poet, Gerard de Nerval, walked his lobster on a blue
silk ribboned leash.
    The lobster, its claws sending   440
        Morse code on the pavement,
            like a blind man's cane, a masked
            rock-heap demanding entrance, a derelict's
            lurching tap-dance in front
            of a bar with closed doors,   445
            whose customers wouldn't break
            their drunken fellowship to come out
            and toss one coin,
    teetered in front of him /   while the onlookers recoiled.
Just that way, i heard,   450

18

my grandmother, five years old,
led her blind grandfather
        through the Galatz Groote Markt,
      linked by a gold-tasseled curtain cord.
He stood on the quay and listened   455
        to freighters, bound for foreign
        cities he'd once known,
        grind down the Danube
while her voice recited   /   the litany of ship's names.

[Dialog of Gerard de Nerval and his Pet Lobster]

Lobster, the poet whispers, so quietly   460
    his voice makes no air stir,
    you are more my friend, my pet,
    my bat, my star, my own true love,
    my Titanic, you, sister, mirror, my soul's widow,
    than any cat or dog might be,   465
    than child or woman or love itself,
    than food or drink or poetry
    which left me starved, used up every
    joy i knew, or my sworn word
    or even that vile dreck, sanity.   470

    Your voice is pure silence, no eavesdropper
    has ever heard it. No bark or myowl
        breaks the still rhythm of my footsteps
        with yours, or cracks my scooped-out skull,
        that cup not made to fill with reasons.   475
        Your claws spread out each side like wings,
        when i lead you through streets where no eye
        drills into me or touches my central pit,
        i can see your deep secrets
    though you tell me nothing.   480

19

Poet, the lobster taps back,
i tell you nothing
because you hear nothing. You are not in an oasis,
nor in Leningrad held together by necessity
in a cruel war, you are in a city where people shrivel terribly   485
for lack of connection. Underground they kill
     for that lack. You think you lead
     me on the end of this dangerous silk. Who's the one
     out in front, and always at the wave's crest, breaking?
I'm dragging you across these currents against your will   490
     like a yo-yo, and you bounce.
One day   /   a ruffian like you will turn his head
     to curse when he feels a woman's eye turn
in the subway car to draw him.
One day   /   an elevator, stalled   495
like you   /   will plunge when a circuit closes
         to call it down.
Like you   /   the storm funnel lifts
         when the butterflies' wings breathe,
     and the starved are dragged by hope of bread.   500
Though you pull back with all your strength
     and dig your heels / into the pavement so hard
         i can see the deep v of the wake
             you leave,
     when the pulse takes me   505
         i reel you in.
When a stone thrown   /   into my mind
         makes ripples,
     i spill you / out   again
     across the Acheron,   510
     hammer you   /   into your dark.
The long worm that pulls you underground through
those tunnels is only a name for me.

8. The Stranger in the City Meets the Ape in the Sky / (The Creature Eats the Monster)

I thought then   /   returned /   stranger to my city,
    of love's power,   515
        i who have known
what it is to lie all night in bed with a carnival
          phantom, a masked bandit,
    to kiss lips that melt at my touch
    from flesh to the cold glass / of a picture, a mirror,   520
    to open myself   /   like a wave, a two-bladed axe,
    and be entered and filled /   by a jet of air, a lie
    that our longing shaped /   not by a passion;

i who have known too in a different city
how nerve can be strung to nerve so strongly   525
    steel cables are less, and an ocean between not break them,
    how bodies once bound, and minds and wills once bound,
    if they hold, when they part can bend all space
    paper-flat, compact all heat to their single measure.

If i didn't love that masked man more than air   530
      (that blotched mask which spreads its wings from his eyes,
    a Rorschach test that takes him with it)
      or water or the pole star's fire,
  i am false coin, or a scooped-out cave
    whose ore has been yanked with forked tongs   535
      to mushroom, malignant, in Aldebaran.

If i ask to take back that emptied bag,
      my youth, or him who dumped it out,
  i am the Frankenstein monster, dumb, split
    coil and recoil, pursued by its own   540
    mad, doubled self across its own Arctic planes
    to its own frozen waste, its blind dazzle.

If i count my losses my own, my spent
        life, my pain, all my own
           mine alone   545
   i am the Creature from the Black Lagoon
        King Kong shaking a blunt paw
           at the bugs that buzz round his dizzy spire,
  and Fay Wray, too, gripped in his hairy fist,
        helpless against that animal stink.   550

[Dialog of King Kong and Fay Wray]

Matted Monarch of the Empire State,
he opens his blunt fist to sigh
a ludicrous, wrenched farewell: *poor fluttering*
butterfly, my pet, my dear,
    my Beatrice-of-paradise, my vulture,   555
    my battleship, my soul, my saucer,
    my Rorschach, my mirror, you, my widow,
     i hold in this purdah, you, fading larva
        whose blood-count's low from poisoned dust,
how you squirm in my hand, arms flopping.   560
    i see you yearn
like invisible light for your liberty.
Though you squeak for freedom, my delicate bat,
    until you undo
       your metamorphosis,   565
     drill back into your pulp,
until you uncoil that labyrinth, that shell
      which hatched you a soul,
    and return to the worm
    you were, in the base court under my heel, 570
    you can't escape my strong force
shaggy cohesion, my brute pursuit.

Monster of sapience, who shake this world
from your spine's spire, on which your brain
mushrooms, a shillelagh, a clenched, clawed node,   575
Fay Wray replies: i am the burning
dust you breathe.
 Before you were born or grew
  dominion from your infant swamp
  the hope of me tattered your black jacket,   580
  four quick slash marks, clean through the lining,
   an epic of tangled streets,
   spoils wrenched from the jungle,
  like AIDS or the possibility of Brasília.
Mold that has grown   585
 skin-deep i can eat off again. I nestle in your palm now,
 spirochete, mutated germ, decaying helix.
My sharp, particular grains corkscrew
 through your membranes into every vein,
  at every shudder,   590
 drill you female to my male
 as they rush through your opening valves
  to your heart's hub. Cesium, i glow
 in your brain / gnaw the desire from the will
Until you come   595
 down from Monarch to bug, from mental tower
 to my base dust, until you spread
 yourself flat in my mud, open to the cleansing
 grains like a two-bladed axe to subatomic rain,
 your farewell is mere boast. Not discrete in Eden,   600
  not pinpointed high in Aldebaran,
 but in the dolphin's gut,
 in a child's heart, in a worm's dream,
in a butterfly's span / you may find your lost
  double, and re-knit hole *to* whole   605
 to healing *to* healed *to* health *to* hale *to* hail
 and, renamed, in that innocence greet me again.

9. At My Own Door

My mind hovers over the board like a surveillance
satellite, re/membering who i am.

You, networks of subways /   who tie the far   610
       reach of Queens to the Lower East Side;
you, hidden, dangerous silks, who bring my daughters home late
nights from no-thoroughfare jobs to the heart's-end terror;
you, webs, hammocks   /   who cradle the hope-starved
child and its used-up mother, back from no-exit,   615
equally in your rocking; you, magnets; you, currents;
underground galaxy, my synapses, my maelstrom:
    tie the sacrificed queen to the hand that plays her out
    for a cause not hers; the mutated germ to the world without
                                   | charity
    or self-preservation that lets it arc; the abandoned cesium   620
    in the obsolete x-ray machine to the man and the woman
    in the dusty village, hungry for a moment that shines
    like an Andean god; eternity to this speck torn from their dust,
    corrupt / poisoned and radiant half-life.

Up Broadway to Harlem to Arbor Hill, what everyone calls   625
       loneliness, i call constellation,
           connection.

To get the name right is not ease but necessity:
like breathing, like coming to the correct address when one's been
                               | invited,
more than a courtesy.   /   Maybe we have to go back   630
       look for the names, start again:
the right place, not Aldebaran or Eden but Albany
              here
              where i am

with lever, winch, cables, nets 635
machinery of connection   my fulcrum, where i stand
                            trying to shift something.
When i press down, it moves
when i pull tight, it holds.

      ---Oct. 28, 1987---Dec. 4, 2004
      ---New York City---Albany

T W O :
THE LAVA TREE

"Comme sur quelque vergue bas
  Plongeant avec la caravelle
  Écumait toujours en ébas
  Un oiseau d'annonce nouvelle..."

---Stephane Mallarmé

THE LAVA TREE

there are griefs that color and freshen the world:
one day we wake to see a field in flower
   the dew on each leaf reflecting our eyes
one day we notice that gold meadow
    which woke all around while we were looking at our hands
    and we turn away from ourselves to smell the new-mown
                                   | sweetness.

there are oaks we watch grow a long time
from their hidden seed:
     the aging of our mothers and fathers
     that day when they leave us
   our own aging, how each day we stiffen, we learn more slowly
   and lose what we learn, how our noon will pass, how our night
                                  | will cover us
   a giant with huge limbs, shading us from the sun.

there are sudden sharp moments that sear the summer:
   without warning they shear us, turn us brittle
   all at once, we know the sudden drying out of friendship
   how those we believed root and branch of ourselves cut us off
   how love itself will wither us, shrivel, betray us.
   consumed, we feel the dry wind flame through our stalks.

there are storms we wait out in stubborn helplessness:
   the fury funnels over our children, bares roots, strips the soil,
   together we bow to the storm, together it passes over or breaks
                                    | us

   though we cannot endure it for them, it is ours.

there are winters of growing coldness, tundras

in which we see that we will never bear, never fulfill our

|promise:

the seed we carried so carefully has lost its season,
love has no more use for us, we must go down into our own

|ice.

and we do go down, we are frozen under, the world endures
its seasons without our generosity, our green good,
without anyone knowing.

granite, smoking lives:
this has happened to me; it has happened to others i love

then that day burns   /   we leap into sorrow again:
that dark flame which filled the earth's heart
uncurls, its tendrils breaking through the fissures.
how well we become that luxuriance, how we flourish,
how we open ourselves, unfold ourselves to that light,
how, air and wash of plenty

we breathe out our lives.

FOR MARGARET, GRIEVING,

1.
Downstairs under the hole
that deepens the front stairs
something is shifting around.

If you go to the cellar
you'll find your life
a microscope you never play with
a doll, a toy mouse
a stuffed bear with no name,
worn smooth from clutching.

2.
Who is the woman in the cellarage
turning, turning in her torn slip?
She's broken, she has no hands.
She can't hold a thing.
Her party dress has no pockets,
her feet no toes
she has no name.

Her head has been winched around backwards on her neck
she sees where she's been,
can't see where to go, who
will hold her.

3.
Jolt, jolt, rock me, bust me, shake me, hit me
again, i'm No-Name, hold me, want me,
my mother's got no
arms to hold me, she can't, she's hurt, all broken, a fix, call me
what you like so you call me

yours, a fix, a fix, i'm cold, i'm spilled
out, my first mother's
lost.

 4.
 A child inside a child
 in a nest inside a child:
 inside you a nest, yourself
 inside yourself, child to yourself:

 says patience, patience; it says don't
 change me, let me be
 what i am, it says how
 can i know, how
 can i breathe
 my life, it's so
 thin

5.
The hungry downstairs
will take you for all you have,
 dream you when you're alone.

Nobody's doll-baby, when you fall down
and spin alone into that mouth,
it will eat your teddy bear.
It will crack
your jaw.

 It will whisper:
 Grief, you are still
 grieving, night's own
 little girl. Don't cry any
 more. I swear you won't be
 wasted. I'll make you

a new dress
a party dress that shifts with the sharks, a dirty dress,
a mother dress.
I'll kiss you till all hurt's
gone / into my dark, my fur
hand womb, my earth
fall pools, i
will dress your bones in love,
and you'll rest

in me

FOR JAMES, IN TIME

Don't say it
don't even think it
that someone will look out
some day at this crystallized light, the glass angles
of snow, these ice marigolds
outside my window,
as i do now, while i take the star down from the tree,
and say how good the world is
without you
in her arms.

Dear James, murdered last year in Thailand, if you were here at my living-room window, twenty-three years old, awkward dandy leaning into your life, with a silk ascot, a paisley handkerchief, patched second-hand tweed trousers, a frightened but determined eagerness, and a glass of wine in your hand, i'd ask you: when we die, do all those possibilities which blurred us

suddenly shrink,
concentrate to a clear pinpoint
like the hole in the mouth of a straw
or the wise men's star? i thought you held such promise
in your defenseless, gay
honesty, your ambition. To take our lives
as themselves, without armor,
without excuse, as you've done, isn't this
the only greatness we can make
alone, for ourselves, even if nobody else
consents?

i didn't guess what you would become, but now you're so soon completed, i stand at the window, sipping iced tea through a straw,

the star in my left hand, and see what you were, shrunken to a clean
dot of light.

> little ghost, almost my child,
> transparent crystal, not yet grown
> into your power, thought-pulse, microscopic
> blot, soul seed so small you could
> fall into the open hole
> at the top of this straw: though i try not to,
> i imagine your last
> moments. Did you clutch with both hands, catch
> at your killer, kick for a foothold,
> before you fell down, through
> your life? You never shirked
> a hard question, but now
> when you're wholly
> imagined, you look past me and sink
> into your full / silence.

No, going down into yourself is not a descent but a naked
focusing. See it plain. In a room whose mirrors bent your reflec-
tion, showed you to yourself, as you thought, wrong-angled, without
grace, you used what you could. Four squares of tofu, a handful of
snow-peas, half a red pepper slivered, four sliced mushrooms, four
shrimp, a sprinkle of dill weed, two ginger curls, two marigolds, one
on each plate, placed carefully, off center, and the best five dollar wine
to be found:

> with these you composed
> not dinner for the two of us but a ceremony,
> an embrace.
> One step after
> another, we pace
> sideways in time, and i think
> what can be saved

When you were eighteen, your first day in my class, surrounded by strangers, you read, with shy determination, expecting the obvious brutalities, a poem about your first love, in Amsterdam. You'd asked a man the way to the tram, and he offered you love; you stayed with him a week. There was neither disguise, nor pose, nor plea for acceptance in your words; you named things clearly.

> If you stood at this window with me
> now, not imagined, my best crystal glass
> in your hand, my arm around your waist,
> i'd say to you, help me
> take down the decorations.
> we're in another place
> we look and then
> we say

i think how much love was still waiting for you. With careful, with ceremonious attention, you would have born witness, as poets do. When would your life have opened its full grace? After you had to put your cat to sleep, you cried in my arms, on the street, your bicycle propped against a lamp-post, the empty carrying case in the basket. The paisley silk handkerchief you'd folded in your breast pocket, so that you'd carry him to his death with the formality you wanted for him, was spotted, cat-drool and tears.

> Here's a silk
> handkerchief
> for your death, folded plainly
> forthrightly, as you could wish.

> It is not unexpected
> after pain

we give ourselves
to simplicity, as you have done,
with no reserve,
just this
and then
just this

QUIET LIFE

1
what should she do with a roomful of hands and feet?
how many years had she bent to harvest the creased
    jeans, to reap the ripe socks
    from the rug, to gather the garlands
    of scarves her daughters had looped
    on chairs or shrugged
    from their arms?
how long to thresh, to winnow, to mill?

always in that frame of early light
with the crash of garbage collectors outside
and the buses roaring, the cars humming through the glass
she felt that other, that visitor in her mind
    that ghost who walked the cluttered rooms
    and was free, who could walk through walls
    who could lie down under cars
    and sleep, then get up unhurt, who could walk through fire
    unburnt, who could live even in the flames
in her mind, and walk out alive
    that ghost who looked like her.

what loveliness, she said to the ghost
in your grey patience
    you've sat winter nights
    eaten storms, and not minded
here lies particular light
    in clutter and hurry, here lies your life
    you carry in your hands
    to give away
    such light
      it tears my eyelids

to a steel fringe

2

will you be glad
when time forgets to speak to you
from the toe of an empty shoe
and the mirror forgets how much it loved you?
    the tape-deck, with a nasty hum, a whine
    crawls into your head
will you laugh
in the changing night that is what you have
will you say   *I shall travel the lizard tide*
    i shall teach the quick chameleon
    to change to something like herself
    to learn to be the thing i am
    and not to seem like what i see?
then count   how many eyes before you die
    how many teeth before you let yourself sleep
    how many scarves and socks before you lie
    down in the jelly where the dead hands lie
    and let your mind be buried deep.

over the towel rack hangs the night
under the bathtub sleeps the night
it is the blank page on which you write
your life   this night
        that showed me my mother's house
          while i slept.

THE CITY IN THE SEA RISES

under the shifting currents my city grew.
my mind swayed with such grief as women know.

why did you make lamia of me, deadly nightshade,
cut your skull cup from my tenderest smile, carve
my fingers to claws   /   spell Hecate in my name?

in the dark of my moon when you creep to my young
grave to draw my teeth /   now cut your hands on them.

these are my crumbling basalt
            towers /   but who wrecked them?

                              poor sweetheart, deadly angel,
here are my red coral, my jellyfish eyes to float
man-of-war tentacles, here
                        is my tongue, my groin, here
                                obsidian pools, glass
                                  shelter and silk
                        inlet, sweet eddies and salt
                              falls, where my cool sleeve
                        invites you, where you may sink
                        into your endless
                                  feast, your paradise

if my corals affront
        or frighten you   silk drawn
                                and falling, think only
that under these smooth waves, that corrosive deep
is your own desire.
think that it has no life but yours.

think that it is
you and no other, no harbor, no black stone Madonna
but you, naked to yourself

        then close your eyes
        love dazed and drink
        deep of the true night
        in the bleached
leprous
      clinging nightmare
       you made of me
     more than your dream
        i give all
     the sweet tides and the salt..

CALL AND RESPONSE

dark mother
lake of earth, when

you carried me out
of the ice pool under
your heart   at the same time
as the doe in the old
song carried her dead
knight   with the same smooth
                                        motion,

into the earthen lake
                                        you ferried me deep
                                        into that hard time when
i held you in my arms   you were shrunken, small
                                        no curled
                                        animal, but a child to be
                                                         |rocked
                                        into your sleep with tears

cracking open the frozen
body that held us both   body that we both held
                                        in that mutual
                                        action, then, at the same time

i carried you through
whitewater to yourself, to the Mother
you had to become   lake of ash, lake of earth
                                        dark mother in your death
                                                         |curled
                                        fawn rocked to my pulse
                                        in that same smooth
                                        motion, i carried myself
and my daughters, i rushed us over   as the doe carried her knight
through whitewater to ourselves   our eyes reflecting the bright
                                        death armor

41

how could i not know
how could i have forgotten
at all times

now i am the Mother

frozen, hurtling
over, where i bear
down, where they in their turn
bear
join

call and response

it is an equal
motion
lake
of ash, lake of earth

my daughters

rush me away all
one, in that same smooth
motion, that shared

act

DARK MOTHER
November 11, 1994

She was never anyone's sweet
    silence, that lady who carried me down
    into my own
        blood; the owl who rode
    her left shoulder, saw
                through the dark, knew
        how to take
        prey, stayed hungry always

        the black-winged birds
    who took it in turns to ride
        her gloved hand, when she cast
        them upwards on
        her cry
         Take Thought, take Memory!
         Let nothing go!
    came back with live
    crying things in their claws

        the tall black
    cats in motion just back
    of each hip, a pride that made
    its own rules, had taken waywardness
        and fed on it

the dog-headed lover
    who held her chariot's reins
    turned left or right at her word
        no other's, and her wolves
    without breaking for breath
        under the lash

strode till their hearts broke

                the snakes of her hair
        never stopped turning, polished
                their fangs on her brow–
                bones, and her breath
                smoking, braided with theirs

                        even her doves were noisy,
        when they cooed, made messes.

Though she gave us suck, clamped
        to her long, pendulous breasts,
                the arrows of waves,
though she gave us our mother
        tongue, forced us to know
        our desire, took our will
        as hers, taught us hunger,
though she struck our hands
        open so that they might close
        to fists, hold tight to our purpose;
though she sang us to sleep in her night
thunder, where we were her anger....

lady of beasts, who let loose the foaming
stars in streams, she was no means to an end,
but her own way, never surrendered.

                Dark mother, first love, who brought me
                forth into fire and musk
                        my terrible harbor,
                        don't quarrel again
                        with the deep
                it wants nothing from you
You were inconvenient sometimes, annoying,

stubborn, broke me often
on your will. Even dying
you gave no quarter.
How i need you now
in my bones

be with me
when i weaken, don't let me
falter. Be with me
when i twist your snakes
in my hair, when i feed my heart
to the owl on my shoulder.
When i let loose
my ravens to soar underground, be
mine as you were your own.
When my lover turns
the wolf face to me, be
mine, as you were your own.
When the chariot hurtles
headlong into the black
crevasse, and cannot be turned, be
mine as you were your own.

It's over, you've won, you can let it go
My dark mother, look how the deep
lays you down in me, how gently.
Tomorrow when I climb
up, a remembered
thing with my hunter's eyes, your tall
cats will run loose at my call

in the world that hunger rules
we were born to bring good news
with our night eyes
our braided snakes, our dark birds,
alert on our shoulders.

THE RETURN

a warm throbbing near my ear, velvet, a motor turning.
a boat, maybe, or an airplane lifting, a rocket, no, fur,
    the grass head pushing against my throat,
burrowing into me, my brown cat, my earth, my night-colored
                                                   | fuzz-brain,
but he's been dead fifteen years, come back now for comfort,
    and a loud crash, or a thump, something landing
from another universe, yanks me up out of the low rumbling
                                                   | darkness,
a cat most likely, because there's no cat on my pillow,
    neither memory cat nor the actual silver-grey
        cat-belly that likes to curl nights
around my head, dream bonnet, tarn helm, extra brain to send me
stumbling downstairs through the separate cold of fingers and
                                                | night, a thud
as i bump into a stair corner, and whatever fell can't be found
now, hours past, i wake under quilts in my own heat, my cat mind
                                                     | purrs,
stretches claws out, catching a strand of sheet near my cheek,
asleep in a whiskered contentment, and he may know if i was only
    carried or if i woke or dreamed i woke
or still spiral on in that grass vessel where my old mind sleeps
    once in a while swimming up through the heat
of graves and the space under sheets to visit dead time,
to caress love remembered, *the softness of my fur nose*
nudging her sleeping throat, wedging into her dreams,
where she lies on her side in my grave, a low snore, the turning over
of a motor, a heart, maybe, or restlessness, endless desire lifting, a body,
no, the rumbling of that earthquake in which the dead in our dream
    helmets and magic carpet coffins return, as i nuzzle
myself gently back into her dissolving sleep, with my tenderness,
my deep growl, as she holds me a while with her earth fingers

46

in the brown fur night that curls around us both
and then lets me go back to sleep in his grass brain, which one
    of us died, which one lives this dead life
i whisper, as he curls round my skull with his gentle smoke,
    his blunt muzzle, his murmur, *as she lets go*
my earth, my grain, my death, my peace, my peace.

THREE:
NIETZSCHE'S DREAM NARRATIVES

"Who will speak these days
If not I,
If not you?"
---Muriel Rukeyser

MAGNA MATER

Her warmth had fallen on silence, in spite of all promises...
rank after rank they bled, according to their caste
each rank a source for the next of savage harvest

the sun didn't break on Her eyes in a newborn crest
of light, the moon wouldn't turn back to guide the night
with its gentleness, the earth hadn't come to rest

under Her feet like a ship lighting on its right
harbor, tied up safe in its slip as She waited.
None of them had heard. The heaviness had not been made light,

the low not raised high, the crooked by no means straightened,
the starved who were always with Her got no bread
from the bloated, the poor who had followed Her to the gate

no passage. The blind, the halt, the lame, those whose red
ulcers oozed, whose rags sucked at their sores,
the brute survivors who stood emptily as the dead,

burning for violence   /   found no healing. Once on the far shore
the strongest turned   /   back to the next Mother's son who
                                                    |prophesied
new scapegoats, fresh blood-lettings, and more---
cities cleansed of the weak-willed. Nobody went about Her
                                                    |business.

THE LOGIC OF TEACUPS

To live the life
of a teacup requires
considerable patience: to wait
endlessly (so it seems) for that one
    moment when we are
    filled, then wait again
    to be emptied, so that
    once again, for that one
    moment, we are filled
                      never to know
whether that emptiness was loss
                    of a purpose or relief
                    from a burden.

A revolutionary teacup, or one that worked
    sex for gain, or even
a teacup whose uneasy gift was
    prophecy, might not choose
    to accept these given limits,
might propose instead an unacceptable logic:
that we wait, say, to be clean (whether burden
                    or mission),
    then wait again
to be dirty, or even that we, though scummed over
    with such enforced
    passivity, dread
those few moments when we become
    elegant, pristine,
    that we forever fear
tomorrow when our lip will be chipped,
    that we then forever remember----
with nostalgia?---no, friends, with the deepest

repentance----those days of virginal wholeness
   we now forever lack.

But meanwhile outside these tempests, these sudden
   reversals, there waits serene
under a countertop or in a supply closet
   in a dark room,
ready when our Dresden moment explodes,
   a saucer with a difference,
whose consciousness is not unlike yours or mine:

   in your deepest hollow,
   dear reader, as in mine,
   lurks a moose
whose antlers, in the right light,
rise and spread over the verge of the cup,
huge, heaping, generous as an oak,

and whose nostrils, whose superb upper lip,
like the lip of a carp in aspic,
   with a supercilious droop,
   soberly, wittily tell
   the life that logic lacks.

HOW IT WAS IN FROST COUNTRY

Ilyana has been having a stormy summer
with her eggplant. Burt is always acting.
The cat almost flew several times this year.
With luck we'll keep him grounded till his eighteenth
birthday. The dog's left hind kneecap was put
in plaster. He hoops. Arthritis has given my mother
a bad crop. Dad started a new moose.
The marketing and systems work will take him
till mudtime, when he'll trade off the whole country
for what it takes.   These substitutions work
for any data. Jack's mom complains of birds
from radiation in the new TV
we tossed her. Thanksgiving, we're skating
to Atlantis. Things are quiet here
in most equations. The sun is a good red,
that will ring true across your death
and mine. The sound of gun shots
fills the north pasture at dawn. Apples come down
when the whales pass over. Cancer
or not, tell Betty, live, from me.

PRESS CONFERENCE

Was it like that? Was it really going to happen?
After such strong starvation? So many delays? Such clusters of
|dreams
deferred? After measuring the need, examining the needy
and pronouncing them fit? After polling the needless
to confirm that they would not be inconvenienced?

The package contained a bomb. While it was ticking
we conducted our study. Before we'd reached a conclusion,
it went off. All around us, the arms and legs of former associates
discommoded us. The damaged were so damn messy,
so inconsiderate. We did nothing in haste. We would not be
|pushed
or pressured into anything foreign, hasty, exotic
or, dare we suggest it, un-American.

Yes, friends, you may quote me.
If this hadn't been a splendid camera opportunity
we'd have appointed yet another committee
to assure you that we throw our tantrums from strength.
As it was we coined at least one telling phrase:
once more onto the beach dear friends, but nobody
hung in there, however tanned, to be true to or with.
They were all out cruising the strip, making their statements
with pattern or hemline, however fragmentary.
Every one of them made the evening news.

Finally, standing on our dignity
with both feet (both of them left feet,
because the right had been blown to smithereens)
and giving nothing away, we called this press conference

to announce that we're going to get the economy moving
|again.
Absolutely, that's what i said. Do you read me?
We're going to take our courage in both hands
(right hands, as it happens) and try the mashed potatoes.
I hope i have your vote. This is a paid announcement.

Was it visitation or prophecy? How can i tell you?
If i made this, was it anything to be proud of?
The cheese sandwich on the radiator says: *no*
we have not forgotten our origins, and we melt
right down to our gooey core at the thought of love
without which we are become as breaking picture windows,
or the clash of automobile horns piercing a blurred horizon.
Was this really what you needed to hear? Or i to say?
We must speak to each other with new mouths or die.

MOONSCAPE

A kind of weariness pursues me
from one corner of the president's eyebrow
to another, so that when i have climbed over
the brow-ridge, and slid clumsily into the hollow where the corner
of the eye meets the nose-bridge,
i cannot even imagine how i am to go on,
how i am to set my feet down, one after the other, pointing,
|generally,
in the same direction, how i am to treat this terrain
kindly, how i am not to scar it with my boot-heels, not throw
trash in its crevices,
how i am to arrive anywhere,
or what to say to that pitted moonscape
when i stop at a place where i can see, can shout aloud:
yes, at last, this,
this was my destination. It was worth the struggle,
the sandstorms drilling us, the camels dying of thirst,
the last of the sled dogs devouring each other,
the weak and the useless pushed off the lifeboat to lighten it,
whoever inhabited this rock-pile before we reached it
exterminated, and three of my companions incinerated at landfall.

i have always wanted to stand in this aimless waste
and pitch my country's flag where there is neither air nor honor
on the ridge of the right nostril,
to proclaim to the farthest reaches of Orion's Belt
and to those clear, eyeless witnesses that surround me:
Look, i have elected my leader.
This vacuous gong, this sounding brass, this blank,
this metallic skin disease is mine,
my trophy.
On this featureless disk i shall build my realm.

DENYING

At one in the morning we denied that it would happen. At two in the morning, denied that it was happening. At dawn in the flushed light we denied that it had happened. Some of us, not my friends, denied that it was wrong. Afternoons as shadows lengthened some denied that it took so many. Always some of us, not my family, denied that full number. Always some of us, not my people, denied the full count. Some sunrises, as shadows shortened, that it took those people. Some sunsets, as shadows reddened, that it took anyone but those people. Always, some of us, not our people, that it took our people. Always some of us, chewing muddy hands, denied that it mattered. Always some of us, that it happened. Always, that it was history. Always, that it could happen. That it was happening. That somewhere in a bursting dawn it was happening. That what happened once could happen again. That it was happening again when some denied it. That it would happen again if any denied it. That it would happen again if we did not deny it. That we must deny it space in our minds. That we must deny it space in our imaginations. That we must root it out utterly from our utterance. That we must deny it morning and noon and nightfall, while we choked on the stench. Deny it space to fall on us again. That unless we remembered it constantly, unless we made everyone remember it constantly, we could not deny it space to grow into a name. That we must deny it space again to grow again. That we must deny it space again and again. Again. Again. That we must deny it so that it cannot come again. That unless we remembered it again we could not deny it. That unless we named it again we could not deny it. That unless we choked our minds with it so that nothing else could breathe there, unless we reckoned up those millions again, unless we kept full count of them to the last shadow, with our muddy hands, we could not deny it. That we must deny it space in history to grow again. That we must deny it again before midnight comes.

SYCORAX, OF HER ISLAND

"...The foul witch, Sycorax, who with Age and Envy
Was grown into a hoop: hast thou forgot her?"
                              —Shakespeare, *The Tempest*

There must be some reason for it, i mutter, bent over in a hoop
rolling along in Times Square under your foot,
my nose right down so i can smell out the price of a meal.
They said i was a lousy mother, and took my dirty brat away,
taught him to shut his mouth, do snot work for snot pay.
Now i don't see him hang around the tunnels where the slick
                                        |squealers squeal
on each other, while he shakes them out from his hair and nails.

Yet, wherever you've hidden him, when he starts to peel
off scum from his shoe, he curses the clean with a razor blade.
If ever he finds where his ma is, he'll cut his way
right back through your smooth face into these arms of mine.
Then he'll open you up, hat to wallet, like a good son,
chop straight through to find me out where i wait,
your hard pellet,
         your green lump you swallowed and can't get out,
                                        your grit.

Look how the gut that made you has turned to air---
and my boy--- i wouldn't know him if he cut me down now.
You're pretending not to see me, walking straight through my ear,
as if you have work to do, and i, when i hear
such brave creatures, such island voices , your footsteps clicking
                                        |along

in front of me, i pretend that i see you, my proud
city, although there's no shadow here but mine,
          although i'm not who you think i am,
                    although you're not there.

THE AURA OF ART

There is an aura, which a work of art has, even while it is dying, which it carries in its arms like a beached whale or a dinosaur egg. The whale rots. Whole villages die of the stench or decamp like a bevy of flies when the strength is gone, in horror of so much flesh beyond use. The dinosaur egg hatches. If the work of art is lucky, the fledgling eats only what it needs of that smoky seizure before taking off for the palisades, from whose rock faces it will repeatedly launch itself like a dragon in search of living food. If not so lucky, that haze, that caloric wobble of magnetism, that luxury, will be devoured down through each atom and out into the anti-matter beyond, and then the work dies. A new life, however, has been let loose, ravenous, rank, completely lacking in decoration, fueled by the lost chromosomes of dead art. We spy on it as it mindlessly lurches through plate glass windows and corset factories. Once, the absent manufacturers might have fit the bones of our dead whale over living matter to give it form, female, male, or otherwise. Now, inside the scavenger's gut in its deliquescing phosphorescence, it perishes dreadfully from lack of weather. Without weather it cannot speak to us. Poor dissolving art, we used it ill.

THE INVASION OF LARK STREET, ALBANY, AFTER THE FIRST BUSH INAUGURATION

They're counting dead women and children over on Lark Street,
  counting parts: here a hand, there a foot,
  counting teeth
        gold fillings,
                there, behind my house.
These people don't belong here. In the deli or in the card store
they have no Right-to-Shop. They must be the dead of some
                                              | other country.
Nobody's issued them green cards. They sneaked in over the
                                              | border
  to steal graves from our grandmothers.

                        No, we won't hunt them down.
        What do you take us for? We're gentle people.
        But before we can grant them amnesty
    Immigration has to count heads. Quietly, quietly.
You, line up, please: gassed here, shot there, disappeared
near the boutique on the left,
            malnutrition in front of the thrift shop.

    Cold January, kind hearts, and efficiency:
we're so busy counting, though, that we haven't noticed
the skulls are all empty: no conversation pits, microwaves, mirrors,
no triple dressers, no shoes, no feet to need shoes. No eyes
look out at us through those wall-to-wall carpetless eyeholes.
Even the ones intact: why, their insides are bleached, walls scrubbed
                                              | down.
The inhabitants checked out long ago. In some other country, not
                                              | ours,

far from Lark Street, they laugh with each other, they walk arm in
|arm
through January's clean summer, leaning against each other,
    leaning into each other
        as if they could find safe harbor in each other,
    as if the fortresses they rotted in never ground their loins to
|rubble,
    as if in each other's bodies they disinvent poisoned air,
    disinvent the explosions that spilled clean laundry
        into the street, that showered
        earthenware, tin cups, that rained
    pump handles, kettles, lips
        down to make glisten the soil.

Look how the season turns, and still no harm done.
In April's silk mistiness, when in other latitudes the leaves fall,
when Albany's melting snows are stroked up from the ground,
    then stroked down again in rain,
        air answering earth in a long caress,
Tulip time, Glorious Fourth, October-Fest, New Year's Eve
the voices of those who never knew tulips on Lark Street
soothe the night. Their arms rock the night to their breasts.
Even the four-year olds croon to their Employer night in tired,
|maternal voices:

    Sleep, sleep my love, nobody knows you're here with me.
    Nobody will take you away. Nobody will find you
    here on Lark street where they don't feel
    how quietly   they are entering the death of time.

SESTINA: WHEN I AM NO GOOD FOR YOU

Tomorrow, let me imagine, your lips will give me some new link
                                     | with reality,
like a prayer, a form of thankfulness, filling quietly as a pail
with rain, with myself and yourself. In that touch, beyond good
                                       | and evil,
no sense will lift or isolate us, no producer of decay
filter us one from the other. We will be the good rain god,
the dark, slick surface of all corners the world over.

When the corners surface darkly, the world over
your lips will keep its link with the rain, guessing reality
is merely a sign, a good weather prediction, not the actual presence
                                       | of the rain god.
We have no forms to thank those who pour us out into the pail
nor the sensate potions, products whose flat decadence
wakes neither you nor me, who age, neither good nor evil

but useless, as myself when i am no good for you. Evil
in all corners would, on the whole, be preferable. It would surface
                                       | the dark world over,
lofty, producing senile mutterings. Its decadence
could coat your lips with chocolate or dark muck as easily as with
                                       | reality
before the old forms of thanks when we are far from each other
                                       | begin to pale.
Don't answer the door now. It will do no good.   It is merely the
                                       | rain god

knocking, merely something from outside, hoping for a good rain.
                                       | The god
has forgotten his former goodness, wants neither your self nor me.
                                       | An evil

and glaring form with eyes, how he hates thankfulness. He is a pail
whose acid surface eats all corners.   In the dark world, over
your shoulder, waits your next contact, lips you, tongues you till
                                        | you shudder. Really,
you must lose or let loose your senses. Without their loft, what can
                                | we produce? Decadence

lifts you but drops you, produces no life, not even senile, not even
                                        | decadent
life. If only you could come to me tomorrow as the good rain
                                        | god,
lip me deep and give me contact. Reality
would be so good, not myself but you as you can be when no evil
surfaces in any dark corner. The world over
we could melt to one form, and each tongue would thank the
                                | other. Each pale

sweat-covered flank would thank the touch that cannot pale,
not go insensate, not lose its loft, profound, laughing at decay,
dark surface that feels out corners.   If we could have the world
                                        | over
again, i would ask no more good than this, merely the love rain,
                                        | god
of remembered wells, selving us into good, into evil
if need be, but at least into touch, lips in real

time, lips that taste real forms and thank each other, with the pail
still to fill, beyond the self's good leavings, sensual, decayed
down to good rain, to surface in all dark corners, the world over.

OBSCENITIES

Holes in a body? What comes out of holes in a body? Liquid, solid, gas, flesh, flame? The flow of the body, the materials of the body, for its own life? Bodies at rest? What is put into holes in a body, if the body wills? Bodies in motion? In the flesh? Fruit, milk, fingers, flesh, things unknown to touch, smell, taste, lava, tides? Frontally? Nude? What is put into holes in a body, if the body does not will, if another body wills, forced into one body if a different body wills? Stripped? On all fronts? Front and back? Water, food, flesh, wood, iron, nails, brooms, gush of disgust, odor of dead clams? Backsides, backsliding? Holes in a body, new holes that are not there until a different body wills? Affronted? Denuded? Backing out? Holes in the throat, the breast, the trunk, through which calendars flow? Eye hole with no eyes, nose holes with no nose? Confronting, then ? Skull scraped, stripped, denuded, emptied out? Who pulled out now, trailing what strings, what gobs? The flow of the body, the materials of the body, not for its own life? Wholes, wholes in a body, the whole of the body, the wholeness of the body, living, in image, in matter, in color and space, in flesh? The whole of the body in its whole body, before us? The whole body in its tides, its swells? The whole of the body frontally or turning in space? Erased? Silenced? Affronted? Heavenly bodies confronting us in their motion? The silence of those infinite spaces, erased? The whole of the body, its gravity, its magnetic pull, its strong force, turning in space? Clouds over the body, seas churning the body, wild fiery nebulae hair and milk of suns? The whole bodies of space, the whole bodies of earth? Blood of stars now gone? Ancient, exploded suns? The bright wholes, the black wholes, their pull on us, their drawing of us, their flow into us, our pull upon them, their pull upon us? Erased? Silenced? Affronted? Which body pulls you into it when i am erased?

PLAIN/SONG

what is there here for us to love
what can we find that we can love

here there is only you and i
before we die, before we die

here, only a piece of bread
only a heel of farmer's bread

only a heavy woolen glove
only a red, a sticky glove

inside the glove a severed hand
the clenched fist of a severed hand

inside that fist a broken bird
the crushed bones of a broken bird

a ragged bird that has no throat
whose scream of steel ripped through its throat

not one who breathes will hear it sing
not quick not dead will hear that song

but all across the windswept plain
dead armies gnaw that barren pain

those yet to count, those yet to breathe
those still to breed, those still to bleed

there, severed hand to severed hand
my bone hand fused to your bone hand

my shadow tongue in your dust mouth
your dust tongue in my shadow mouth

where silent bone that counts the wrong
will ring with flame our shrunken song

there, in the flame sheets, you and i,
each time we die, each time we die

will shudder out that victory song
till all who breathe know right from wrong

STONE OLIVES

(In Memory of Melina Hudson
and those who died with her in the bombing of PAN AM 103)

Tulip-flowered wind, night-smelling sea,
long swell of desert sands, and the roar of tractors
crawling up from the Hudson, from under water
into Albany's Washington Park: what is that plowing?

>It is the sound
>>of olive trees.
First one, then two, then the whole grove, they drop
>>their small, hard fruits
and their tears are gathered up,
packed into baskets, then carried
to the earth-floored rooms.
>>Some go into jars.
Some have their centers plucked out
to be filled with slivered almonds or roasted
>>red peppers. Some go to the press
where they're crushed. From their pulp
oozes the purest gold,
>>to be strained into jars and sold.

>*Little dead ones,* they sing, *blink blink,*
>as they fall, *little dead ones, blink blink*
>*la muerte, ay, los niños, ay, la muerte.*
Take my hand, come down, dance with me, take my hand.

Tulip-fluttered wind, night-swelling sea:
in the smell of desert sands, before we were born,
the tractors ploughed back time from under Mount Sinai
into Washington Park. There, carved stone

Moses watches his wise God stand hard by
as the father prepares to spill on the quickening sand
his son. No olive trees whisper here. Does Abraham
see that no scapegoat waits at hand? His son
    and his son's sons and daughters,
sucked down, will sweeten that sand, no matter how many
small, innocent, wordless furs squeak out their lives.
What is dying now, even as we speak, to save us?

        It is the stand
    of apple trees behind the barbed wire.
  First one, then two, then the whole grove, the sun
      flattens them. Gravid, they droop,
      ripen, and men lean ladders,
and their treasures are gathered, packed,
      into baskets, then ferried out
    from the earth-walled rooms.
      Some are rendered down,
    some peeled of their skins, grated
with almonds, and mixed to haroseth that makes sweet
the bitter herbs. Some have their teeth plucked out
for the fillings. Some go to the press.
From their pulped flesh oozes the purest gold,
sweeter, oh Lord their God, than the fruit of the vine
to be filtered through cheesecloth and sold.

Little dead ones, they sing, *shalom,*
as they drop, *little dead ones, shalom*
ich sterbe hier, nicht versteh, je crêve, nou verbeshti, mamaye.
Take my hand, come down, dance with me, take my hand.

Tulip-sequined wind, night-shimmying sea,
long bloom of desert sands, and the roar of the spring
festival onto the grass: tell me the mother,
before our history sprouted, should have thrown

herself under the blades to save her child. Yes, tell me
the father should have given to God the Father
his own life, not his son's. Tell me, if all,
man, woman, child, had thrown their lives away
rather than take that dumb, furred sacrifice
still squeaking its lives out under our knives
would all our history have borne different fruits?
We planted no orchard here next to City Hall
but the walls still shake. What are we plowing under
    when we do that prime time shimmy?

       It is the sands
        of the pyramids.
   One grain, then two, then whole stones, they melt.
     Their sharp, unlanded granules
drill from their homeless camps the far away dam.
The wind lifts them, gathers them in, and they ride
      the red tide's maternal breast
from their hulled earth rooms to their ghost of a promised land.
    Stones fall, whole shoulders drop
      from the Sphinx who was raised
      by forced labor. Eyes run
   from their heads. Scalps, halves of scalps rain down.
     Melina, who once danced
at proms far from Beirut, laughed with my daughter
years after Hiroshima broke into flower, told
her beads in a church the Gulag never touched,
      now pours down through our air
her young hands full with the seventeen pressed years
      that are all she can hold
      of spring: will the Dead Sea
grow fat with these fragments?
   Our mouths are being stuffed
with our sons and daughters, our centers plucked out
     with tongs. From our poor,

pressed through heat, through cold
over vents and gratings, flow simples, poultices, tinctures
to be forced into jars and sold.

Little dead ones, they sing, *vshh, vshh,*
as they drop, *little dead ones, vshh, vshh.*
d d d kkkkk d d d kkkkk   aaaaaaah heart
Take my hand, come down, dance with me, take my hand.

Tulip-grinning wind, night-crying sea,
long shudder of desert sands, and the drowned tractors
bubbling up from our bodies, cut from our tongues
deep into Washington Park where Moses holds
his law in his hands: they told me God Himself
gave His Son's life to stop it as Abraham
gave Isaac. But what if each father
should give himself? What if we all stand up,
we, who are old enough to have held our lives,
and empty out, not our children, but ourselves?
Why do I hear no such plowing?

Instead, I hear the bend
beyond the asteroids bleed.
First one, then two, then whole planets they fall
and their milk will be pressed out,
their hulled tears, neither water or salt, hold elements
we can neither measure nor read
their red shift to name. They carry
no life we know as life in their milled earths.
Their centaurs are long gone
replaced by an airless patience,
their languages hot ores,
or frozen metals.
Of their forgiveness nothing remains, not even Aztec
gold to be ferried away

to the galaxies and sold.
                              We know what their silence says

Little dead ones, they sing as they shimmy, *aaah nnnnn,*
        as they drop, *little dead ones, aaah nnnnnnnn*
        eiaa mohʃrden, aiee, eiaa khilʃderin, aiee, eiaaaa mohʃrdenn
        nnnnhh   *aaaaaaaaaaaahhhhh.*
Take my hand, come down, dance with me, take my hand.

CODA:

"Bienheureuse la cloche au gosier vigoreux
Qui malgré sa vieillesse, alerte et bien portante,
Jette fidèlement son cri..."

(How fortunate the strong-throated bell
Which, in spite of its age, alert and confident
Throws forth its cry)

----Baudelaire, "The Broken Bell"

AS IF I WATCHED LATE LAST NIGHT
WITH BAUDELAIRE

as if marbles had mouths instead of fitting into them
as if they rolled out sounds
as if i spoke from a stone's heart

        stone orator

        stone orderer

as if crossing the causeway i felt the old cobblestones tell

    what they had known

    of measure, although the cobblestones were not there,

    the roadway cement and tar, the legions not there

    who had made Europe one bell rung to their tread

as if my mouth lay, one with the roadbed, a cobbled rock

        throbbing to their heels

    myself earth's rock heart under the road

    a buried sweep of rock, a plate of rock

    so many miles its curve held measure, not sight,

    a huge, dull, rock globe burning to their heels

as if a fault line split me and i rang

    yes, dead friend, i have wasted my life

    buried that one talent underground, cracked, dead

    so it rings dull now, harsh now, won't test true

        eaten with earth and water

        ordure, not order

            spilt

    with caring for what gave no care back

as if sea-bed and crag cracked through and i stuttered, yes

    fifty ill-fitted years and fitfully worked

    i've lost the best of it, not found what matched me,

    loved, loins and loyalty, and not been loved

    and my children's sweetness meets different needs, not that.

see the ghost legion break its march on the ghost road

cement and tar over a memory net of cobbles
cloven in the bleak, shifting plates that groan
with their ghost step
                    this stretched globe, my mouth
although they walk through meaningless pain to their deaths,
have died, holocausts with them,
they're breaking the march with a dice game;
                    odds are, that fire, joy
hope of embrace encircling me in love not hate
has just rolled down on the ghost stones in ghost dice
and the luck's gone with their lilt, roll,
                    splash / the lift of the language

as if the rock plates pulsed and swelled
                    and the earth through that cracked hell-mouth
                    shot streamers of fire and stone,
                    shot ribbons, shot looping spirals, fired the Crab
                    Nebula, Andromeda, Ursa Major,
as if out of that mouth
                    a wild galaxy of fire and rock whooped
                    riotously through me as i lay heaped
                    under its domed, ribboned net, its laced spears
                                        and rang, yes,
                    whatever i have left to make the best of
                    is not what i should have made ,and small time to do it,
                                        (yes, sisters, for sure
                                        i blew it)

as if the rock beneath and the dome above were one bell of fire
                    and swung the life away
as if i were the clapper, the small, hard tongue of that bell,
                    and the bell itself, and my fellow legions who lay
                    cowering, groaning, believing the bell cracked
                    when all the while it gave out its clear shout
                    joy and assent from a whole heart, itself and you,

yes, even for you, lover or liar, late into this vigil,
    reader or sleeper, wherever you are, my ghost legion,
        you, like me, broken and still free and hale
as if we could praise each other forever in this world.

NOTES:

<u>Note on poetics for "Sestina: When I am No Good for You"</u>:

This sestina was made by choosing the six words that ended lines 1, 15, 25, 41, 54, and 66 (lines chosen at random) of section 15 of Whitman's "Song of Myself." and linking with each of these, one set for each end word, rearrangements and variations of phrases taken from sentences in section 15 and following of Nietzsche's "The Anti-Christ." Because those sections have long sentences but not many, I counted from the first of section 15, and through the next three sections to get sentences 15, 25, 41, 54, and 66 sentences after the first. The resulting linkages, which were then treated as internally variable units repeated in the pattern of the sestina, were:

  1. lips—contact with reality;
  2. form of thankfulness—pail;
  3. myself—beyond good and evil;
  4. loft—senile product of decadence;
  5. rain—merely the good god;
  6. surface—the god of all the dark corners...the world over

<u>Notes to "Stone Olives"</u>:

Wasington Park, Stone Moses: In Washington Park, Albany, Melina Hudson's city, there stands an imposing stone fountain with a statue of Moses striking the rock.

la muerte, ay, los niños, ay, la muerte: Spanish; death, alas, the children, alas, death

ich sterbe hier, nicht versteh, je crêve, nou verbeshti, mamay: various languages; I'm croaking (dying like an animal), don't understand, I'm croaking, shut up, mommy

eiaa mohſrden, aiee, eiaa khilſderin, aiee, eiaaaa mohſrdenn: hypthetical dead language from 'beyond the galaxies'; alas, death, the children, alas, death

Notes to Cities of Mathematics and Desire:

Major Sources:
Guillaume Apollinaire, *Le Chanson du Mal-Aimé*
Anna Akhmatova, *Poem Without a Hero*
James Gleick, *Chaos*
Gary Zukav, *The Dancing Wu-Li Masters*
Douglas Hofstadter, *Gödel, Escher, Bach*
King Kong

Poetics:
I began this poem with arbitrary decisions first to counterpoint an argumentative or musical structure drawn from Apollinaire with rhetorical constructions drawn from Akhmatova, and then to write automatically, rejecting nothing. The assumption was that chaos=complex order. Although the images that arose seemed to me at the time random, I later determined that they were in fact topologically related, since the hoodlum, mask, suspension bridge, ape, butterfly, lobster, labyris, etc., are all bilaterally symmetrical objects and can be transformed one into the other without breaking the outline. Their bilateral symmetry probably reflects, as a counterpoint rather than an illustration, my concern with a linguistic structure common to both Apollinaire and Akhmatova, which might be put as "not a but b." Both poets assert that we are not here but there, that the name is not this but that, that "if I didn't love you well I am not myself but something else." These rhetorical constructs, unlike the lobster, etc., are not bilaterally symmetrical because the positive term does not name, contain in itself, or call to mind the negative term, while, on the other hand, the negative term is always forced to name, contain in itself, and call to mind the positive term. Absence must express itself by naming some other thing as a presence, while presence names itself (not x names x; x names itself but does not name not x). This quality in language I propose, in this poem, to be somewhat analogous to spin in physics, or to the structure of the helix in DNA.

Line notes:
Poems weave themselves in conversation with all of the art, and therefore exist, not in an individualized vacuum but in a textual matrix. I assume, perhaps incorrectly, that the parts of my matrix that link to French and Russian poems or to the vocabularies of science or magic may be less

familiar to some American poetry readers than my links to poetry in English. While this material is not necessary for understanding, I'm noting some of it for pleasure below.

1. Wargames
Line 1: "one night last year..."
Apollinaire, "Le Chanson du Mal-Aimé" opening stanza:

> "One night of light fog in London
> A roughneck who looked a lot like
> my sweetheart bumped into me
> and the look in his eyes hit me
> so hard I looked down in shame."

I give this in my own version because that's what I used; the best translations of Apollinaire are by William Meredith.

Line 3: "I caught from the corner of my eye..."
Hopkins, "The Windhover": "I caught this morning morning's minion, king / dom of daylight's dauphin, dapple-dawn-drawn falcon in his riding..."

Line 14: "the purple bruise over his eyebrow..."
Apollinaire:

> "It was that inhuman look
> the scar on the bare neck..."

Line 23: "his distant frown, like a surveillance / satellite..." Apollinaire:
> "...the wise Ulysses'
> old dog recognized him,
> near a thick carpet where his wife
> kept watch for his return."

Line 27: "singularity...fine excess..."
Keats: "Poetry should astonish not by singularity but by a fine excess..."

Singularity: the point at the center of a black hole, in which an object will be squeezed to zero volume (Zukav); the point in its curve at which a mathematical entity behaves abnormally.

Line 33: "Could make the Neva rise / to whisk you away from a death-trip street-gang"
Akhmatova's river, Leningrad/ World War II, Stalin's purges.

2. Of the Power of Chess...
Line 45: "of rainbows..."
Elizabeth Bishop's "The Fish:"
>   "---until everything
>   was rainbow, rainbow, rainbow!
>   And I let the fish go."

Line 60: "Like answers like...Because the sky is a net...you are caught,"
etc., a central theorem of magic.

Line 83: "the lost don't come / like Akhmatova's..."
In "Poem Without a Hero," the siege of Leningrad and thereafter, the poet is visited by figures in masquerade costumes, the ghosts of former companions from the city's pre-revolution days as St. Petersburg.

3. Of the Power of Maps...
Line 87: "I thought then of love's power, I who have known..." The use of this repeated stanza is one of the structural elements from Apollinaire:
>   "I who know heroic songs for queens,
>   the lamentations of my spent years,
>   hymns of slaves in the swamps,
>   the romance of the unloved man,
>   and songs fit for sirens to sing."

Line 88: "in bed with a carnival / phantom..."
Akhamatova's masquerading ghosts.

Line 101: "You, networks of subways..."
The use of this repeated stanza is a second structural element from Apollinaire:
>   "Milky way, oh luminous sister
>   of Canaan's river
>   and the white bodies of our lovers,
>   drowned swimmers, can we follow, breathless,

your course to other nebulae?"

Line 102: "dangerous silks, who bring my daughters home late..."
Sappho, (tr. Willis Barnstone):
"Hesperus, you bring home all the bright dawn disperses,
bring home the sheep,
bring home the goat, bring the child home to its mother."

Line 114: "the Neva's swirling smoke..."
Akhmatova (tr. Kunitz and Hayward):
"the Neva smokes beyond the window,
the night is fathomless, and it goes on and on---
this Petersburg bacchanalia."

Line 119: "the cesium...in the x-ray machine..."
In 1987, the inhabitants of a village in the Andes thought this radioactive dust in a medical waste dump beautiful and sacred, so coated their bodies with it and ate it, with predictable results.

4. The Flight of the Monarchs
Line 181" ...in small bursts..." photons, in quantum theory.

Line 188: "Though you've come to the Hudson, not the Neva..."
Akhmatova (tr. Kunitz and Hayward):
"You've come to the wrong place,
the Doges' Palace is next door..."

5. The Scholars of Chaos
Line 225: "world-shifting Archimedes..."
who said "Give me a long enough lever and a place to stand, and I can move the world."

Line 228: "the Doges' Palace.../the marshes....the Groote Markt..../Dimension outside time and space/...crystals /...amber /...not the Lethe...but my own city..."
For this string, see Akhmatova (tr. D. M. Thomas; this section not available in the Kunitz and Hayward volume):
1)"Not on the cursed marshes of Mazur,

Not on Carpathia's azure
Peaks---in your own house!"
2)"...you were both in a dimension
    outside the laws of space and time---
    there, in what polar crystals,
    and in what amber glister
    at the Lethe's--- at the Neva's---mouth."

Line 245: "number of the arc/...measure the heavens..."
Sir Thomas Browne:

> "...that masse of flesh that circumscribes me, limits not my
> mind: that surface that tells the heavens it hath an end,
> cannot perswade me I have any; I take my circle to be
> above three hundred and sixty, though the number of the
> Arke do measure my body, it comprehendeth not my
> minde: whilst I study to find how I am a Microcosme or
> little world, I finde my selfe something more than the
> great."

Line 265: "written in invisible blood..."
Akhmatova (tr. Thomas):

> "...at least one crime: I write
> In invisible ink, and light
> breaks only when it's reflected..."

Line 269: "as mirror to image, as self / to double, as nature to temple,"
etc.. This string is made from:
1) Akhmatova's construction of her poem around a series of doubles,
2) her recycling of Baudelaire both directly and as recycled by Eliot in
The Waste Land:

> "You, hypocrite reader, my mirror image, my brother...."
3) Baudelaire, in "Correspondances:"

> "Nature is a temple where.../
> .../perfumes, colors, and sounds answer each other."

Line 276: "the great Russian poet and her son...prison...slaughter," etc.
Akhmatova herself, and her son, separated when he was imprisoned by
Stalin, as she recounts in "Requiem."

Line 282: "angle of incidence...angle of reflection..."
Optical law about light reflected in mirrors: the angle of incidence equals the angle of reflection.

Line 328: "I fanned...with a butterfly's wing, as my scholars tell..."
Gleick: a metaphor about weather formation in chaos studies.

6. Sheba's Apron:
Line 340: "particles/ whose speed and location burn equally beyond my graph..."
My magnification or breakdown of the uncertainty principle (that either speed or location may be known but not both at the same time). Here, nothing is known.

Line 345: "furiously escaped..."
John Crowe Ransom in "The Equilibrists, " about bodies in Heaven: "In Heaven you have heard no marriage is / No white flesh tinder to your lecheries / Your male and female tissue
sweetly shaped / Sublimed away and furiously escaped."

Line 350: "negative inversion..."
Auden:
> "Sir, no man's enemy, forgiving all
> But will his negative inversion, be prodigal..."

Line 355: "Do we truly believe that they mirror each other..."
Zukav: about the behavior of subatomic particles in split screen experiments.

Line 386: "...not the Palace of Golden Bulls.../ but my own home," a compression of:
1) "not the Neva," and "not the Doges' Palace,...but---in your own house...", above;
2) the prologue to Akhmatova's "Requiem" (tr. Thomas):
> "No, not under a foreign heavenly-cope, and
> not canopied by foreign wings---
> I was with my people in those hours,

84

There where, unhappily, my people were."

Line 362: "...El Greco Cucurucu Angel..."
This compression is made from:
1) Akhmatova (tr. Thomas):
> "If an angel had stooped in its flight
> home to El Greco's heaven..."
2), Cucurucu: character in Peter Weiss' *Marat/Sade*.
Line 365: "...bowels like sour air..."
Apollinaire:
> "your mother let loose a juicy fart
> and you were born from her colic cramps..."

Line 367: "Zaporoguean Cossacks,"
Apollinaire:
> "I'm faithful like a dog
> to its master, like the vine to the trunk,
> and like the Zaporoguean Cossacks,
> foulmouthed, pious, and drunk,
> to their steppes and their decalogue."

Line 371: LeRoy Breunig: my teacher in 1956, and author of <u>Guillaume Apollinaire</u>, Columbia University Press: New York and
> London, 1969.

Line 377: "...the stanzas the censors cut...white space whose voids blaze..."
Akhmatova, where Soviet censors cut sections of "Poem Without a Hero," did not make substitutions or close up the gaps, but instead left numbered blank stanzas, thus making that enforced silence speak. Hence, those stanzas were indeed "written in invisible ink."

Line 386: "love itself sat down at the board..."
Apollinaire: "The falsity even of love itself..."

Line 389: "No, I am not Sheba's lethal apron..."
This compression is made from
1) Akhmatova (tr. Thomas):

"...I am not that English muse,
not La Belle Dame Sans Merci;"
2)Akhmatova playing off Eliot's Prufrock: "I am not Prince Hamlet nor
was meant to be,"
3) elsewhere in the poem (possibly the translators have substituted this for
a Russian allusion, or possibly the Russian allusion also played off the
same line) she plays off Hamlet's "What's Hecuba to him, or he to
Hecuba" with "What to me are Hamlet's garters?"

Line 390: "...from whose strings Nerval hanged himself..."
Nerval hanged himself with an old apron string, which he carried with
him and had told his friends was "the Queen of Sheba's garter."

Line 405: "stagger out of a tavern, drunk..."
In Apollinaire's poem, a drunken woman who staggers out of a tavern
reminds him of his lost love.

Line 413: "a mask and a stone glove"
The statue of the Commendatore, from Don Giovanni, inviting the
doomed libertine to dinner in Hell, is one of the masked guests to visit in
Akhmatova's poem; its knocking becomes first the hammering on the
window and then the clicking in the throat, in the section quoted below
(note to line 441).

Line 414: "the rebound from the future..."
In Akhmatova's poem, the guest from the future is reputed to be the
scholar, Isaiah Berlin, who had visited her in Russia. Based on this for-
mulation of hers, throughout this poem I revise Newton's law that every
action produces an equal and opposite reaction, to assume, instead, that
every action and its apparent response are generated at the same instant,
implicit in each other and united as one event.

Line 426: "I am here, in my house,"
Akhamatova, "Poem Without a Hero" and "Requiem," noted above.

7. In the Palais-Royal...
Line 427: "If ever I forget.../let my feet turn"
Apollinaire:

"Let these brick waves fall
If you weren't greatly loved
I am the Egyptian king,
his sister-wife and his army
if you weren't my only love."

Line 441: "claws sending / Morse"
Akhmatova (tr. Thomas) (see note to line 413, above):
"...WHAT IF, SUDDENLY, THE THEME ESCAPES
AND HAMMERS ON THE WINDOW WITH ITS FISTS,---
ANSWERED BY DISTANT, DREADFUL SOUNDS---
A CLICKING IN THE THROAT, A RATTLE..."

Line 461: "Lobster...my pet,"
Nerval said that he liked his pet lobster better than a cat or a dog because
it didn't meow or bark, and it knew the secrets of the deep.

Line 465: "..my bat, my star... my sister,"
This string is made of
1) Akhmatova (tr. Kunitz and Hayward):
    "...You will be my widow.
    O my dove, my star, my sister!"
2) Akhmatova, playing off Baudelaire's "my mirror image, my brother," as
she does elsewhere in her poem...
3) Baudelaire, in "L'Invitation au Voyage,"
    "My child, my sister,
    think of the sweetness
    of going to live there together.../
    in the country that is your mirror..."
4) Apollinaire:
    "Let me never forget her
    my dove, my whiteness,
    my daisy whose petals have been pulled off,
    my distant isle, my promised land."

Line 465: "my Titanic"
A compression of:
1) Apollinaire:

"my beautiful ship, o memory
haven't we traveled enough
through this undrinkable sea?"
2) Rimbaud's boat in "Le Bateau Ivre."

Line 475: "my scooped-out skull..."
Nerval carried a skull with him to use for drinking

Line 484: "You are not in an oasis/...you are in a city where
people shrivel..."
Akhmatova: "not in the Doges' Palace" and "not La Belle Dame Sans
Merci," above.

Line 511: "across the Acheron..."
Nerval, referring to his returns from the madhouse: "Two times, victorious, I crossed the Acheron..."

8. The Stranger in the City:
Subtitle to section 8,"The Creature Eats the Monster":
Parody horror film title from a 1950's Sid Caesar show.

Line 531: "If I didn't love"
Apollinaire, passage on Egyptian king, quoted above.

Line 538: "If I ask to take back that emptied bag"
Apollinaire:
"If ever she returned to me
I'd say to her, I'm happy now."

Line 571: "...in the base court..."
Shakespeare, Richard II:
"In the base court? Come down? Down court! Down king!"
I'm indebted to Susan Howe, *My Emily Dickinson*, for her discussion of
the asymmetries in this play.

Line 571: "my strong force / shaggy cohesion..."
Physics: the strong force, one of the forces of nuclear cohesion, one of the
four hypothetical forces that hold the universe together.

Line 603: "..in the dolphin's gut,"
Akhmatova (tr. Thomas):
> "...How admiringly you'd have watched me
> as in the gut of the dolphin
> I saved myself from the shark..."

9. At my Own Door:
Line 626: "Arbor Hill"
Albany ghetto neighborhood, equivalent of New York City's Harlem.
"what everyone calls / loneliness, I call constellation ..." Akhmatova (tr. Thomas):
> "She alone leans over me,
> she whom people call spring
> I call loneliness."

Line 629: "To get the name right is not ease but necessity."
In magical poetics, knowing the inner name or the true name of a thing gives the mage power over it. In contemporary times, a similar magical poetics shaped the political actions of the 1960's. Both the Black Power movement and Feminism, for example, built large parts of their rhetoric on changing the demeaning names given their populations to names of their own choice, which act gives the speakers power over their own natures and their destinies.

BIOGRAPHICAL NOTE

Judith Emlyn Johnson began her career imagining that she would be a composer of operas, and considers her poetry in print to be the score for a form of spoken opera or spoken oratorio. She is the author of two books of short fiction and nine books of poetry, the first of which, *Uranium Poems*, won a Yale Series of Younger Poets Prize in 1969. Among her other awards and honors are a Playboy fiction award, a National Endowment for the Arts Poetry Fellowship, and, for "Cities of Mathematics and Desire", the Poetry Society of America Di Castagnola Prize. She has served as President of the Board of Associated Writing Programs and as President of the Poetry Society of America. Currently, she edits the feminist literary periodical, *13th Moon*, and publishes *The Little Magazine*, now an electronic journal. She is Associate Dean of Undergraduate Studies and Professor of English and Women's Studies at the State University of New York at Albany, where she has chaired both her academic departments.